# Start Your Proofreading Side-Hustle

*Maximize Your Writing Skills*

## Ashan R. Hampton

Cornerstone Publishing
Arkansas

Cover Design: Ashan R. Hampton
Cover Photo: © *Can Stock Photo* / *Kakigori*

**Websites:** www.arhampton.com
www.prowritingskills.com
www.startproofreadingnow.com

**ISBN-** 978-1-077-54526-7

Printed in the United States of America.

First Edition.

Cataloging-in-Publication Data is on file with the Library of Congress.

10 9 8 7 6 5 4 3 2 1

# Proofreading Power Training

**:: Online Classes::**

Proofreading Power

Core Grammar Essentials

Business Grammar Essentials

**:: Books ::**

"Proofreading Power Skills & Drills"

"Proofreading & Grammar Drills Workbook"

**www.startproofreadingnow.com**

**www.arhampton.com**

# About the Author

Ashan R. Hampton has worked as an English instructor for over 20 years, most notably at HBCU Morehouse College in Georgia. She is also a proud graduate of the *Donaghey Scholars Program* at the University of Arkansas at Little Rock under the direction of Dr. C. Earl Ramsey, Emeritus.

Ashan's original research, *History of the Arkansas State Hospital 1859-1930*, was published in the *Pulaski County Historical Review* (1995), and continues to be cited by history scholars today. Her articles on notable African American Arkansans also appear in the *Encyclopedia of Arkansas History and Culture*.

With her doctoral studies on hold, Ashan has found success in online education. She produces and teaches her own writing and grammar courses for global audiences through her small business, Onyx Online Education & Training.

Visit her website: **www.arhampton.com**.

# Other Titles from Ashan R. Hampton

**Adult Learner Grammar Essentials**
(ISBN: 978-0-359-69282-8)

**Grammar Essentials for
Proofreading, Copyediting &
Business Writing**
(ISBN: 978-1-387-91413-5)

**Proofreading Power: Skills & Drills**
(ISBN: 978-1-387-95472-8)

**Proofreading & Grammar Drills
Workbook**
(ISBN: 978-1-716-64564-8)

**Student Success Grammar Skills**
(ISBN: 978-0-359-60763-1)

**Urban Grammar Quick Fixes**
(ISBN: 978-1-329-91923-5)

See a complete listing at
www.arhampton.com/books

# Contents

# Introduction

Proofreading is a booming business, and makes for a great side-hustle or second income, especially for teachers. The push for content marketing has created more opportunities for people with above average language skills to bankroll their knack for words into a profitable small business enterprise.

From solopreneurs to large corporations, more people are blogging, creating email campaigns, newsletters, and all kinds of marketing content to expand their personal and professional brands. As a result, an increased number of writing errors get published all over social media and a variety of written documents. Important documents like contracts, billboards, menus, dissertations and self-published books.

Now more than ever before, the stage is set for good proofreaders to sharpen their skills and market their services. The field of freelance proofreading is wide open with potential personal and business clients everywhere. However, only those who are willing to hustle, sell themselves, pitch and land clients will eat the spoils, and benefit from a pervasive deficiency in writing skills that currently plagues educational and business sectors.

*So, this book answers the question, "How Do I Get Started?"* for job seekers, college students, retirees or active freelance writers who are curious about offering paid proofreading services.

## The Importance of Proofreading

- Mistakes in written documents create a poor first impression. For example, individual job seekers can miss out on interviews and employment opportunities due to mistakes in writing samples, cover letters or résumés.

- Businesses can lose credibility, clients or money due to poor writing and editing mistakes in their written documents.

- In work settings, many employees must write without assistance. Unfortunately, most feel unqualified to correct their own writing.

- Even experienced writers and editors must practice good proofreading skills to produce error-free writing.

## What is Proofreading?

- **Proofreading** is the final stage of the writing process.

- **Proofreading** involves polishing documents by correcting all text and formatting errors before print or distribution.

- **Proofreading** involves making minor changes, additions or deletions to documents.

- **Proofreading** does **NOT** include revising or rewriting. These are copyeditor duties.

Important documents, especially in the workplace, should be proofed by a trained proofreading professional.

# Proofreading Warm-up

**Directions:** Find and correct all **nine (9)** errors.

Did somebody tell you practice made perfect? Thats only if your practicing it right. Each time you spell a word wrong, you're 'practicing' the wrong spelling. So, if your not shore how to spell the word, find out, then practise that spelling. Keep an ongoing notebook of works, so you've got your own personnel dictionary and you can see your progress. Start small, howwever!

*Answers on page 22.*

For more exercises, get your copy of *Proofreading Power Skills & Drills: Become an Effective Proofreader.*

(ISBN: 978-1-387-95472-8)
www.arhampton.com/books

# Chapter 1

# Your Job

## The Job of Proofreader

Proofreaders generally engage in light editing and the correction of general errors with no rewriting.

Basically, hiring a proofreader means the client's document demonstrates decent sentence structure, and acceptable usage of standard English.

For more information on becoming a paid proofreader, consider taking online training classes at **www.startproofreadingnow.com.**

## What Do Proofreaders Check?

Although the client and proofreader determine the scope of services, proofreaders generally check for the following errors:

- Capitalization
- Formatting
- Grammar & Mechanics
- Numbers
- Punctuation
- Spelling & Usage
- Visual Images

## What to Proofread

Although anything written can be proofread, the following list offers examples of the kinds of documents that businesses and individuals typically seek proofreading services for:

- annual reports
- articles
- blog posts
- brochures
- business proposals/reports
- dissertations
- employee/corporate manuals
- executive summaries
- form letters
- general correspondence
- grant proposals
- instructional materials
- legal contracts
- marketing materials
- newsletters
- non-fiction books/novels
- résumés/cover letters
- sales letters
- student essays
- thesis papers
- web content

# Chapter 2
# Your Training &
# Qualifications

Why should anyone pay you to correct their precious written documents? What experience do you have as a proofreader? Are you a good writer? Do you have a portfolio of articles that you have written or edited?

Although a college degree is not necessary to become a paid proofreader, you do need a fair amount of direct training and experience to convince clients to hire you.

## Likely Proofreading Candidates

Usually, editors, writers, teachers, publishers and other professionals from newspapers, magazines, television or news radio stations launch their own freelance proofreading businesses to increase their time-money freedom. Instead of slaving away at an eight-hour job, the ability to work remotely from a flexible schedule is appealing to many workers. Current college students and recent graduates with excellent writing and editing skills might also consider proofreading as a side-hustle. English majors are preferred, but anyone with masterful language skills from any discipline can also become a good proofreader with the right training.

Of course, public and higher education teachers are highly desirable candidates for proofreading, as long as they demonstrate strong writing skills.

Remember, being a teacher or having a college degree does not equate to being a good writer or proofreader. The art of proofreading requires a high level of skill, training and practice. Depending on your industry or current profession, you might need additional training as a proofreader.

So, if you are considering launching a proofreading business, you need to invest in your professional development by taking online classes, and consuming reputable grammar and proofreading books.

To jumpstart your proofreading training, consider joining **The Proofreading Power Academy** at **www.startproofreadingnow.com.**

## Your Skills

Are you good at catching mistakes in your own writing, as well as others? Are you already a good proofreader? Do you have a degree in English or have you completed sufficient training? These are important questions to answer, because your skills and quality of work will determine the success of your business as a proofreader.

As the proprietor of a proofreading service, your job is to ensure accuracy in grammar, spelling, mechanics, punctuation and style for clients who employ your services.

## General Proofreading Essentials

- Grammar
- Mechanics
- Punctuation
- Spelling
- Usage
- Format

## Academic Proofreading Essentials

- American Psychological Association (APA)
- Modern Language Association (MLA)

- The Chicago Manual of Style (CM/CMOS)

- The Kate Turabian Style (CM/CMOS)

## Your Edge

Although you might elect not to service academic clients, you still need to broaden your appeal as a proofreader as much as possible. Doing so might require you to stretch into industries you have not previously considered.

In lieu of a college degree in English, Journalism or another communications discipline, you will need work experience, on-the-job-training, skills training certificates, and good client referrals to make it as a proofreader.

Get certificates in grammar and proofreading to show potential clients and employers, which will certainly bolster your résumé.

Enroll for these online professional development classes at **www.startproofreadingnow.com** or **www.arhampton.com**.

## Your Aptitude for Proofreading

- **Proofreading** requires intense, focused concentration.

- **Proofreading** requires extreme attention to detail.

- **Proofreading** requires persistent focus on tedious amounts of information.

- **Proofreading** requires confidence in English language usage.

- **Proofreading** requires sitting in the same spot for at least 20 minutes at a time, if not hours.

After considering these attributes of proofreading, your skills, aptitude, training and qualifications, do you think you have the ability to meet the demands of proofreading? Do you have the right attitude toward proofreading?

Is this something you actually like to do? Before creating an entire business around proofreading, honestly assess your ability and willingness to turn this side-hustle into a profitable enterprise.

## Answers: Proofreading Warm-up

Did somebody tell you practice **makes** perfect? **That's** only if **you're** practicing it right. Each time you spell a word wrong, you're 'practicing' the wrong spelling. So, if **you're** not **sure** how to spell the word, find out, then **practice** that spelling. Keep an ongoing notebook of **words**, so you've got your own **personal** dictionary and you can see your progress. Start small, **however**!

For more exercises, get your copy of the *Proofreading & Grammar Drills Workbook.*

(ISBN: 978-1-716-64564-8)
www.arhampton.com/books

# Chapter 3
# Your Skill Level

Did you know there are different degrees of proof-reading, ranging from beginner to senior? What level of proofreader are you?

Determining your skill level as a proofreader will determine what services you can comfortably and realistically offer as a freelance proofreader.

| | |
|---|---|
| **Beginning Proofreader** | Catches errors from the original copy; misspellings, incorrect math, incorrect word/paragraph breaks, typing errors, page numbers and simple formatting errors. |
| **Intermediate 1 Proofreader** | **Beginner duties** plus **advanced spelling** (like homonyms and homophones), and **punctuation** errors. |

| | |
|---|---|
| **Intermediate 2 Proofreader** | Beginner and Intermediate 1 duties plus **grammar** and **mechanics.** |
| **Intermediate 3 Proofreader** | Beginner/Intermediate 1/ Intermediate 2 duties plus usage, academic styles, proofreading marks, galley proofs and simple printing press specifications. |
| **Senior Proofreader** | Beginner/Intermediate 1/ Intermediate 2/ Intermediate 3 duties plus copyediting skills. |

# Chapter 4
# Your Hustle

Now that you understand the expectations of a proofreader, and have weighed your qualifications and skill level, it is time to consider the business aspects of profiting from your proofreading side-hustle.

The next pages and chapters of this book will help you clearly answer these important questions:

- What exact services will I offer?

- What will I be doing?

- What is my niche?

- What will I need to start?

- Who will my customers be?

- How much should I charge? *$50.*

- How will I find clients?

Write down your responses. Consider the answers to these questions as your side-hustle snapshot, a concise look at how you will organize and operate your freelance proofreading business. Remember, freelancers are actually small business owners.

Although you will more than likely work alone as a sole proprietor without additional employees, you must begin to think like a business owner when marketing your services.

## Survey Your Hustle

Yes, you must ask yourself more questions. You bought this book to understand how to turn your proofreading side-hustle into a business. Getting clear within yourself on the effort this will take is the first most essential step for any entrepreneur.

Before you start ordering business cards or office furniture, ask yourself these critical questions:

- Do you have unique knowledge or training?
- Do you like meeting new people?
- Do you have sales skills?
- Do you know how to market your services?
- Do you like helping others?
- How motivated are you to create and launch your own home business? (Rate yourself 1-10).
- Are you willing to spend numerous hours promoting your business before receiving any money?
- Is proofreading an activity you enjoy?

- Will you consistently promote yourself?

- Are you clear on how you can make income from your proofreading services?

- What experience do you have running a small business?

- What guidance do you need to run a small business?

- What challenges or limitations do you face?

- What hours or days do you prefer to devote to this part-time business?

- What skills have you already developed that you can offer to clients right now?

- What additional knowledge or training do you need?

- What financial resources do you currently possess to start your business?

- What tools and equipment do you already own or can get easily?

- Where will you look for customers?

- What is your motto or attitude toward your customers?

- What will be your hourly rate?

- What primary products or services will you offer?

- How many hours will it take you to complete each service you offer?

- What supplies or materials will be required to complete each project?

- Will you charge by the hour, by the page, by word count or by an all-inclusive, flat project rate?

- How many available, billable hours will you devote to proofreading each week?

- What time is available to you to operate this business (days, evenings, or weekends)?

- What do you know or need to know about your potential customers?

## Essential Hustle Reminders

1. **Know your business:** You must know more about this industry than your clients and competitors. Be sure to thoroughly educate yourself on pricing, delivery and all the ins and outs of being a paid proofreader.

2. **Know your customers:** Who are your most likely customers? What do they want? In order to succeed as a proofreader, you must assess the needs of potential clients and service them better than anyone else offering the same services. Who needs your skills? Why? When? How much will they pay? The more you know about your customers, the more clients you will land.

3. **Provide additional value or bonuses:** Other than proofreading services, what added value can you provide customers? What bonuses can you offer to get more clients and to stand out against your competition? Create a product that is not time consuming or taxing, but significant to your customers, such as discount coupons for future services, an exclusive eBook or monthly newsletter.

4. **Aim for referrals:** Actually, instead of always looking for new clients, you want to establish repeat customers who will refer others to

you. This will only happen if you provide five-star professional service with every project. To this end, you must find ways to improve your current services, and ask customers about other related writing or copyediting services they might need.

5. **Keep learning:** Remain teachable and open to learning new skills. Since you are always a student, always find opportunities to invest in your professional development.

Do you have a copy of *"Proofreading Power Skills & Drills: Become an Effective Proofreader"?* This book serves as a low-cost introduction to proofreading.

If you are fired up about proofreading, and are ready to seriously train with the intentions of starting a freelance business, try online classes that offer certificates of completion.

Get all of the details about proofreading books and online classes at:

**www.startproofreadingnow.com**

**www.arhampton.com**

## Check Yourself

- Are you still interested in paid proofreading?

- Are you ready to start your own proofreading business?

- Do you need additional training?

- Were you confident about your proofreading side-hustle, but now you are not sure?

**Write your thoughts...**

_____

_____

_____

_____

_____

_____

## Proofreading Warm-up

**Directions:** Find and correct **seven (7)** errors in this brief passage.

I see that your have taken *the* bathroom tille *tile* to the garage. When can you *finish* furnish the job? My open house gala is in a few days, and I must impress the guests. Can you get more workers hear to compleate the job quick? *here*

*Answers on page 40.*

For grammar and usage refreshers, get your copy of *Grammar Essentials for Proofreading, Copyediting & Business Writing.*

(ISBN: 978-1-387-91413-5)
**www.arhampton.com/books**

# Chapter 5
# Your Initial Essentials

What do you need to get started? Are you confident that proofreading is a good fit for you? If you are ready to take the leap into freelancing, you might be ready to start gathering your resources. Along with outlining the basic operations of your home business, you also need to assemble the minimum supplies needed to get started.

## What exact services will you offer?

An example answer to this question might sound like this: *"I will proofread document text, and offer to correctly format academic parenthetical and bibliography citations in APA and MLA format only."*

This means you will proofread and correct each document for grammar, mechanics, punctuation, spelling, usage and formatting errors as previously discussed. You will also format research citations.

For instance, if an academic customer provides reference information within the body of the paper and on the reference page that do not meet the requirements of APA or MLA, you will format these citations, in addition to proofreading.

So, according to this example, you will offer two services: 1) General Proofreading and 2) Academic Citation Formatting.

## What will you be doing?
## Workflow Scenario

What will be your workflow in accepting and completing proofreading assignments? How exactly will you begin and end a proofreading project? Perhaps you will check your Gmail account from your home computer everyday at 7 a.m. to see if any clients have contacted you.

If so, you will reply and tell them you have received their document. You will review it and send an invoice with a flat rate dollar amount. You will also mention a turnaround time for completion, such as the next day before 5 p.m. Eastern time or in 48 hours at 6 p.m. Central time. If the client accepts, they pay the fee and you get started proofreading their document.

You print a copy of the client's document and start correcting it with a red pen while sitting at your dining room table. You set a timer every 30 minutes to take a break and to track the number of billable hours you spend on the document. After correcting the printed copy, you return to the computer to open the digital version in Microsoft

Word. You carefully use track changes in red font to transfer the printed copy corrections on to the digital version. Meaning, you find an error on the printed copy. You locate that particular error on the computer copy and insert the correctly spelled word. You do this for every error you find on the printed copy.

Once you have inserted all corrections on the computer copy of the document, you accept all changes to create a clean copy, and you save this corrected version under a different file name. You print the clean copy to see if you missed any additional errors. Once you have successfully fixed every error, you return to your home computer to email the client the finished products.

You will attach the tracked changes version to the email, as well as the clean copy, and send it back to the client. If the file is longer than five pages, you might want to send the completed documents in two different emails. You have now completed your first proofreading job! Record and print your work process in bullet points. Post your workflow and reference it for future proofreading assignments.

## What is your niche?

Perhaps you will only proofread for college student essays. Maybe graduate student writing like theses and dissertations are a better fit for you. You might decide to only work with non-profit groups on their grant projects. Instead of proofreading everything, narrow your area of focus, which makes it easy for potential clients to know exactly what you do and who you serve.

## Who will your customers be?

Once you have established your niche, you can quickly and confidently identify your customers: undergraduate college students, graduate students or non-profit organizations.

## How much will you charge?

Before you decide your prices, research the current proofreading rates through reputable freelancing associations. Your experience and qualifications determine whether you can charge on the low end or higher end of the pricing scale.

For example, let's say the current proofreading rates are $25-$60 an hour; $2-$5 per page or $6-$8 for every 1,000 words. First, you must decide which unit to charge by: hour, page or word count.

Let's say you prefer flat rates and want to charge by the page.

If you have worked as a college English instructor for 20 years, and have published many articles and books, you will charge $5 per page. So, for a 15-page graduate research paper, your fee will be $75. On the other hand, if you are just starting out, you will charge $2 per page, and your fee will be $30. As you can see, background and experience equals more money.

## How will you find clients?

You need paying customers. How will you get them? Perhaps you can afford a small ad in a local newspaper or publication. Maybe you can talk to graduate school administrators about offering your services to students. You might have a strong social media following or maybe you can leverage your LinkedIn profile to attract new clients. Until you build a steady flow of patrons, you will spend the majority of your time marketing your services in the most effective way possible.

## What will you need to start proofreading?

The following list focuses on what you personally need to complete proofreading assignments. The next chapters will detail how to set up your small business.

## Startup Supplies

- Gmail account
- Microsoft Word
- a comfortable chair
- a comfortable table
- collegiate dictionary
- computer (desktop/laptop)
- computer printer
- grammar books
- internet service
- red ink pens
- thesaurus
- white copy paper

Mobile devices, tablets or notebooks will not work for proofreading. Your computer should have a large enough screen for ease of reading.

If you cannot afford Microsoft Word, use similar free, open source word processing software that uses the .doc or .docx format. Although you can access a dictionary and thesaurus online, it is still best to purchase a current printed version for your home office. What happens if your internet goes down? For grammar and proofreading resources, visit **www.arhampton.com**.

## Check Yourself

1. What exact services will you offer?


2. What will you be doing? Outline your workflow.
   - 
   - 
   - 
   - 
   - 
   - 
   - 


3. What is your niche?


4. Who will your customers be?


5. How much will you charge?


6. How will you find clients?


7. What will you need to start proofreading?

**Answers:** Proofreading Warm-up

I see that **you** have taken bathroom **tile** to the garage. When can you **finish** the job? My open house gala is in a few days, and I must **impress** the guests. Can you get more workers **here** to **complete** the job **quickly**?

For a comprehensive grammar overview, get your copy of *Adult Learner Grammar Essentials.*

(ISBN: 978-0-359-69282-8)
www.arhampton.com/books

# Chapter 6
# Your Business Setup

Remember, freelancers are small business owners. In order to turn your side-hustle into a profitable small business, there are steps to take with your state and local governments to legally operate your home business.

You must also register with the federal government for tax purposes. But, do not worry. The process is easy, especially for sole proprietors, which is the focus of this chapter, not LLC's or Inc's.

- Your Business Name
- Your Business Name Registration
- Your Business License
- Your Tax Identification Number

## Your Business Name

Choose a professional sounding name for your freelance business. Unless the name is extremely unique, you might be surprised at how many other companies already operate under your choice of company name.

For example, *Cornerstone Communications* is quite common in several states across the nation. However, you could try *Cornerstone Proofreading and Editing* or *Cornerstone Writing Services*. To make sure no one in your state or county has already registered your exact company name, run a search through your Secretary of State's office.

In the state of Arkansas, you can conduct a "business entity" search from the Secretary of State's home page. Search all corporation types and fictious names, if your state provides those options.

If a similar name, but not the exact name, such as *Cornerstone Communications, Inc.* pops up in the search results instead of your choice of *Cornerstone Communications*, please choose from your alternate titles to avoid confusion or potential lawsuits. In this example, *Cornerstone Writing Services* might be a better option.

At some point, you might want to expand into freelance writing or copyediting, so make sure your company's name allows for that kind of growth, instead of specifically branding it as a proofreading business.

## Your Business Name Registration

In some states, you do not have to register your business name with the Secretary of State as a sole proprietor. You can simply obtain a business license under your company's name. However, since the requirements for each state differ, you must research your state's process for business registration and licenses.

In the state of Arkansas, anybody who wants to start a business must contact the Secretary of State's Business & Commercial Services division. In their online publication called, "Doing Business in Arkansas" (p. 4), the responsibilities for filing a business as a sole proprietorship read as follows:

> **Sole Proprietorship.** A business with a single owner with no formal or separate form of business structure is known as a sole proprietorship. The owner has sole control and responsibility of the business. A sole proprietorship is easily formed, allows important decisions to be made quickly, and typically has fewer legal restrictions. In this situation the owner and the business are indistinguishable. 4 The business has limited life and cannot be transferred (as an entity) to others. **Generally, paperwork for sole proprietorships is NOT filed with the Secretary of State; some is filed at the county level.** The sole proprietor's responsibilities include but are not limited to:
>
> • Obtain all capital.

- Incur personal liability for all debts and claims against the business.

- Claim all profits and losses on the owner's personal income tax return.

- Obtain state and local business licenses and permits.

- Record the name of the business with your local county clerk.

So, in the state of Arkansas, sole proprietors do not need to register their company names with the Secretary of State. Make sure to research the rules for the state in which you are establishing your business.

## Your Business License

In some states, you might have to apply for a business license at your local city hall, court or county clerk's office. Fees can range from $25-$50 or more. In the state of Arkansas, the business license form also carries conditions for home-based businesses. Since freelancers typically use a room or a small portion of their living space to complete assignments, be sure to file and apply as a sole proprietor, home-based business.

## Your Tax Identification Number (EIN)

As a sole proprietor, home-based freelancer, your company is associated with your social security number. Most freelancers identify their business names by using the acronym D.B.A., which stands for "Doing Business As."

So, on your personal checking account, your name should be listed *as Ashan R. Hampton, D.B.A. Cornerstone Writing Services*, for example.

Instead of listing your social security number on invoices, checks or other financial statements, apply for an Employer Identification Number (EIN) from the federal Internal Revenue Service (IRS).

For detailed information on the EIN, search and download publication number 1635, *Understanding Your Employer Identification Number (EIN)*.

**https://www.irs.gov/pub/irs-pdf/p1635.pdf**

You can easily apply for the EIN online. From the IRS.gov homepage, type in the search phrase, "Apply for an Employer Identification Number (EIN) Online." After completing the application, your new EIN will arrive by email.

## Your Bank Account

As a solo business owner, it is not necessary to open a separate checking account. However, you might still choose to funnel your personal and business transactions into separate accounts.

Whether you update your current account or open a new account, you need to add your D.B.A. company name. This way, if clients write checks for your services, they can make it out to you personally under your name or under your D.B.A. name. However, for tax purposes, you will still file under your personal name and social security number, not your D.B.A. name or EIN.

If you have any concerns about paying taxes as a part-time or full-time freelancer, please contact the IRS directly, or consult with a certified public accountant or another financial services advisor.

## Accepting Online Payments

Since you will conduct business online via email, you need to establish an online payment method. PayPal is the world's leading online invoicing and payment system that most clients recognize and trust.

Therefore, you need to create a PayPal business account, if you have not done so already. If for some reason you are opposed to using PayPal, then choose another reputable alternative.

Do not rely on CashApp or similar mobile, money transfer services to receive payments. Remember, you must record your financial transactions in the most effective way possible.

## Contracts and Invoices

Some freelancers use invoices as a contract where they list the services being provided and their fees. However, if you want to require a separate, simple contract for services, (in addition to an invoice), that is signed or digitally initialed by the client, feel free to use both options. The internet is saturated with contract templates for freelancers.

## Reference Books

Since it is impossible to know everything, as an editing professional, you will spend a good deal of time researching grammar, usage and style issues.

At minimum, you need the current versions of the following reference books:

- Webster's New World English Grammar Handbook

- Merriam Webster's Collegiate Dictionary

- The Associated Press Style Book

- Grammar Essentials for Proofreading, Copyediting & Business Writing

# Pro Writing Skills Online Classes

## Business Grammar Essentials

The online class **"Business Grammar Essentials"** is the ultimate, convenient, cost-effective online solution to quickly boost your workplace writing skills. Learn to identify and correct usage and style issues commonly found in business documents.

## Core Grammar Essentials

**"Core Grammar Essentials"** helps you to improve your writing for personal and business success. This class covers the most troublesome grammar errors for beginning and professional writers.

## Proofreading Power

**"Proofreading Power"** introduces the fundamentals of proofreading through practical exercises and quizzes. You must have strong grammar skills to successfully complete this course.

Add **"Grammar Essentials for Proofreading, Copyediting & Business Writing"** to your reference collection.

**ISBN:** 978-1-387-91413-5
**www.arhampton.com**
**www.prowritingskills.com**

# Chapter 7
# Your Home Office

After legally structuring your home-based freelance business, it is now time for the fun part! Setting up your workspace. You can keep it simple or splurge on designer furniture and decorations. Either way, you must feel comfortable and productive in your office space.

Establishing a home office is emotionally and psychologically rewarding, because it makes you feel like a legitimate business professional. Even if you work in pajamas, entering a dedicated office within your living space enforces the idea of work in your mind, which increases the likelihood of you completing assignments without distraction.

Unlike Chapter 5, "Initial Essentials," that offered suggestions for startup proofreading supplies, this chapter includes additional necessities and niceties to round out your home office.

## Your Desk & Chair

Position your desk or work table and chair in a comfortable area within your home for easy access to electrical outlets and telephone jacks.

(Yes, some internet service providers still use old school telephone jacks for routers and VoIP.)

## Your Computer

A modern computer is the most important piece of equipment you will own. You cannot function as a freelance proofreader without continuous access to a computer.

Unfortunately, using public computers in libraries or café hubs will not suffice. Fortunately, desktop computers and laptops are inexpensive. Nowadays, you can purchase a good, high-powered desktop computer for less than $300.

Since most clients probably create document files on PCs with Microsoft Word, use your dollars to purchase a PC with the latest Microsoft Windows Operating System. You can easily convert Mac files on a PC. However, since the Apple system is so proprietary, it is difficult to convert PC generated files on a Mac.

If you can afford it, purchase a desktop and a laptop for a combination of flexibility and backup. Laptops are portable and allow you to work from almost any location in the world. However, for storing client files and adding peripherals like a larger monitor, desktops are best.

**Computer Monitor:** Since you will spend an exorbitant amount of time working from your computer, purchase the desktop or laptop with the largest screen size available or that your budget will allow.

**Printer:** Printers are inexpensive and extremely necessary to any proofreading enterprise, since you must print documents of varying page lengths. Although inkjet printers are available for less than $40, the refill ink cartridges can cost more than that, so price the ink before purchasing the printer.

Color printers or laser printers are niceties, but not necessary for your day-to-day operations. Both are a bit more expensive than inkjet printers.

For example, you might catch a color laser printer on sale for less than $300, but the toner cartridges often cost $80-$150 per cartridge.

**Scanner:** Many all-in-one printers come with built-in scanning capabilities. As a proofreader, you will occasionally need to scan and convert documents. If a client submits a document as an Adobe PDF file, the scanner Optical Character Recognition (OCR) tool can create text, which can be copied and pasted into Microsoft Word or a similar word processing program. At other times, you might need to convert a hard copy document into a digital format that can be easily transmitted through email.

**Fax:** Believe it or not, some companies still use fax machines to conduct business. Since all-in-one printers include fax capabilities, purchasing a separate fax machine is unnecessary. Make sure to choose a printer unit that allows for wireless faxing, otherwise you will need to use a phone jack to activate this feature.

## Your Telephone Service

Many freelancers use their personal cellphones as business phones. To save money, this is a viable option. However, if you frequently engage in client phone consultations or teleconferencing, you might want to invest in landline phone service, since spotty reception often plagues wireless cell service.

If you want a separate vanity business number to avoid directly distributing your personal number on business cards or other marketing materials, Google offers a free alternative to adding a business line to your current phone service plan.

**Google Voice:** This free VoIP service offers a list of available numbers within your area code. Once you choose a phone number, you can forward calls from the Google Voice number to your personal cell or home phone. This way, you can filter business calls from personal calls.

## Your Internet Service

High-speed internet is a must for any freelancer. As a proofreader, you will spend lots of time on the internet conducting research, looking for clients, and sending documents back and forth to your customers. Cable internet is generally more reliable than satellite, but the monthly fees can get fairly expensive.

If you are just starting out, you can use the mobile hotspot feature through your cellphone provider to power your desktop or laptop for brief stints of time, depending on your data package. You might also use free wi-fi at local libraries, cafes or retail stores as a temporary fix. Eventually, as business picks up, you will need to invest in secure high-speed internet.

## Your Email

Use a professional email address! Do not conduct business with questionable personal addresses like *prettylady1908@yahoo.com* or something as equally horrendous. At the time of this writing, Gmail addresses are acceptable in lieu of a dedicated business email address. Certain email extensions seriously date you, and harm your ability to attract technically sophisticated clientele. Think aol.com., sbcglobal.net, compuserv, msn or hotmail.com.

## Your Software

As a proofreader, you will use Microsoft Office programs the most, since their software dominates the business world. Even if you primarily use web-based email, *Outlook* offers calendar and reminder features that might be helpful.

Also, free email providers or open-share software files might display unprofessional advertisements or watermarks on your documents, so...beware.

Microsoft Publisher only makes the list, because a church or small business might use this program to produce a newsletter that needs proofreading. Out of all of the available programs in this suite, you must purchase or somehow acquire Microsoft Word.

Adobe software products domineer document creation and distribution in the workplace. You must purchase a monthly subscription to Adobe Acrobat to create and send PDF files. If you use a free alternative, make sure the program allows you to create, edit and comment on PDF files, not just open and read them.

Accounting and anti-virus software are the least sexy of your software toolkit, but both are quite necessary to the launch and expansion of your proofreading business. Also, familiarize yourself with Dropbox, Google Drive or a similar program for sending and receiving large files that cannot be attached to an email.

**Essential Software:**

- Microsoft Word
- File Sharing (e.g. *Dropbox*)
- Antivirus Software
- Adobe Acrobat (PDF)
- Accounting Software

**Optional Software:**

- Microsoft Publisher
- Microsoft PowerPoint
- Microsoft Outlook
- Microsoft Excel (Schedules/Finances)

## Office Supplies

Who doesn't like buying office supplies, especially during back-to-school sales? Stock up on these office supply basics:

- white copy paper
- sticky notes
- stapler/staples
- printer ink cartridges
- paper clips
- legal pads/small note pads
- highlighters
- file folders
- black, blue and red ink pens
- binder clips

## Office Niceties

- address labels
- book cases
- bookshelves
- clocks
- decorative pillows
- decorative rugs
- desk or floor lamps
- envelopes
- file folder organizer
- file folders
- filing cabinets
- floral arrangements
- folding chair
- folding table
- manila envelopes
- mouse pad
- plants
- ruler
- wall decorations
- wireless keyboard
- wireless mouse

# Chapter 8
# Your Website

Yes, you absolutely need a website! Every small business owner, side-hustler or entrepreneur must invest in a website, because potential customers expect it. Your website is your calling card, so it must be professionally designed and well-written.

With the recent proliferation of *do-it-yourself* website builders, establishing a business website is not as expensive as it once was. As a proofreader, your website is essential for attracting new clients and maintaining repeat customers.

Luckily, you do not need an expensive or fancy website to launch your proofreading business.

You only need a simple **three-page** website:
1. Home page
2. About/services page
3. Contact page

In this website structure, you could place full contact information on the home page, and use the third page for a blog or samples of your work. You can creatively mix and match these three pages, depending on your personal preferences.

Remember, the goal of hosting a website is to convince people to hire you and compensate you for your services.

## Choosing a Web Designer

Hiring a web designer is tricky, because the process can turn into a total nightmare, if you are not careful. Typically, web designers create and own your materials, depending on the scope of services in your contract.

Unless you include a work-for-hire provision in your contract that gives you rights and access to all of the website materials, you cannot simply expect the designer to hand over the content files if you decide to discontinue services or hire someone else.

Owning the files will cost you more money, but it might be worth it in the long run. The designer might also require a hefty transfer fee before providing you access to the website content. So, get a clear understanding of how your designer handles transferring and cancelling services.

Please be advised that your website content does not automatically include your domain name. For example, let's say that a designer has linked your site to www.editplenty.com. You love this website address and want to keep it as long as you are in business. In a worst-case scenario, a petty designer might reluctantly hand over your content files, but refuse to transfer your domain name from their information to yours. If this happens, you will need to choose a new domain name for your business. Again, clarify how the designer handles domain transfers if he or she goes out of business, or if you simply want a new website with a new designer.

If this is the case, you want to be able to transfer your current domain name to your new website. Even if you want the designer to shut your site down without giving you the content, you still need your domain name.

However, if you want to start fresh with a totally new website and a completely new domain name, then you are in good shape! You do not need anything from the designer. You can simply discontinue services and allow them to shut the site down.

## What You Need from a Web Designer

You do not need a WordPress site! Avoid these like the plague! WordPress sites are unstable, need frequent maintenance, and are difficult to revise with simple changes like replacing an image or posting a new article.

Instead, you need a designer to build a website in a user-friendly content editor like Wix, so that you can maintain the site yourself by adding or deleting content. This also makes it easier on the designer, because choosing and revising a template is much faster than creating original source files in Dreamweaver or Photoshop.

With this website design method, your site can be up and running in three days, but certainly within two weeks.

## What Your Web Designer Needs from You

Before you approach a web designer, you must be clear on how you want your site to look, the titles of your three pages that will appear in the menu bar, and the content you want posted on each page.

- A homepage template or design idea
- Titles of your 3 web pages
- Content for each page

If you do not provide the written content for each page, the web designer will probably charge extra for copywriting services. If the designer does not provide this service, you will need to find someone else to write your web content.

At minimum, the web designer and the copywriter need the following information to get started on your site:

**Home Page:**

- What main header image do you want? Your personal pictures or stock photos?

- What written content should appear on the home page? Slogans?
- Do you have a logo?

**About Page:**

- Your bio.
- Your company story (how you began).
- Staff bio (if applicable).
- Pictures of yourself, business location, staff or stock photos.

**Products / Services:**

- What do you sell?
- What services do you offer?
- Do you have pictures of your products?

**Contact:**

- Company name and or your personal name?
- Address?
- Phone number?
- Email address?
- Do you want a map?
- Do you want a contact form?

## Choosing a Domain Name

- Choose a professional web address for your business website.

- Do not try to be clever or cute, just keep the name short and sweet.

- Avoid confusing or alternative spellings.

- Remember, people must type your domain name in their browser navigation bar.

- Do not try to stuff SEO keywords into the name: www.freelanceproofreaderinla.com.

- Instead, you could simply use a portion of your name: www.cjohnson.com.

- If you want to include your service, try something like www.cjproofreading.com.

## How to Get a Domain Name

If at all possible, purchase your domain name through your web hosting provider. For example, if you use *Wix* to create and host your website for a monthly fee, go ahead and buy the domain name for your site through *Wix* as well.

Doing so will save you lots of headache! This way, you can create your site, host it, and connect your domain to the website all in one place. However, if your website hosting platform does not sell domain names, you must purchase one from a separate domain name provider. There are several such companies. GoDaddy is popular, but not necessarily the best domain registrar.

Once you choose a domain registration company, here is what you will do:

1. Go to the domain provider's website.

2. Type your domain name into their search database to make sure it is available.

   If the name is not available, you can choose from closely related alternatives.

3. Make sure your domain name provider is compatible with your website platform, so that you can easily connect the domain address to your website.

4. Purchase the domain name.

5. Find your domain provider's instructions on how to connect and forward your new domain name to your website.

6. After about one hour, type your domain name into a web browser to make sure your website pops up. If not, you will need to contact domain support to properly connect the name to your website.

## Web Design Fees

To get a business website up and running for your proofreading hustle, you will pay for 1) **website design,** 2) **site maintenance fees** (unless you DIY–do–it–yourself), 3) **copywriting services** (unless you DIY), 4) **monthly web hosting fees,** 5) **initial domain registration fee,** 6) after your first full year of service, an **annual domain registration fee.**

Price wise, here are some approximate amounts for each service:

- **3-page, no frills website:** $500–$750 (base rate)

- **Site maintenance fee:** $50–$75 per update or revision

- **Copywriting services:** $85–$150 per page

- **Monthly web hosting:** $9.95–$18.95

- **Domain registration:** $3.95–$16.95

## Important Website Reminders

- Thoroughly research your web designer.

- Unless specified in the contract, you do not automatically own your website content files or access to your domain registration.

- To save time, provide as many photos and written content to the designer as possible.

# Chapter 9
# Finding Customers

Are you ready to find customers? If you have read this book straight through, then you have delved deep into the recesses of your soul to thoroughly consider the business and personal costs of turning your proofreading side-hustle into a legitimate small business venture.

**To review, we have discussed:**

- your proofreading opportunities

- your job as proofreader

- your training and qualifications

- your skill level

- your hustle or motivation

- your startup supplies

- your business tax structure

- your business licenses and registrations

- your website

- your domain name

At this point, if you are still reading this book, you are dead set on starting a proofreading business! Congratulations! Now that you have everything all set up—from your office space to your website—let's get your first paid proofreading assignment.

Unfortunately, customers will not just fall into your lap or serendipitously find your website on the internet. You will need to exert some effort into finding your first few customers.

- Start by telling your friends and family.

- Inform your current and former co-workers of your services.

- Make an announcement to your church, sorority/fraternity, your civic or volunteer organizations or professional associations.

- Tell your hair stylist, barber and everyone you know who can either use or refer your services.

- Post and share your services on your social media accounts (e.g. Facebook, Instagram or Twitter).

- Go through your current email contacts and old collections of business cards from past networking events for new client leads.

## Your LinkedIn Profile

Every business owner must create and maintain a well-crafted LinkedIn profile. This is not optional. When people Google your personal name or company name, they expect to find your website and LinkedIn profile.

No exceptions. Business professionals, recruiters and potential clients regularly use LinkedIn to survey your background, work samples and skills.

If you do not have the time or inclination to complete your profile, (which could take several hours), look for freelance writers who offer this service, especially résumé writers.

Begin your LinkedIn journey by creating a new account at **www.linkedin.com**.

If you already have a LinkedIn profile, update the information and add work samples to entice people to read about your background and patronize your services.

## Leverage Your LinkedIn Profile

In the headline underneath your photo, identify yourself as a freelance proofreader. In the about section, briefly tell the story of how you began proofreading. Include your skills, your services, certifications or unique professional experiences.

As you begin to appear in search results, potential clients can read a synopsis of your professional background and the services you offer.

- Make your profile active with recruiters who might be helpful in finding remote contract work.

- Search for proofreading jobs on LinkedIn. You might find part-time or contract listings. Even if a company posts a full-time position, you can still offer to support its team by freelancing, until the position is filled.

- Take time to post useful information about proofreading, share articles, tasteful memes or personal work/client stories that drive potential clients to your website.

- Publish articles on LinkedIn. Share your expertise on proofreading or other related subjects of interest to business professionals.

For example, an article on cleaning up your social media presence before job searching can garner hundreds of views to your profile, and hopefully to your business website.

At the end of the article, mention that you edit résumés and cover letters. Provide a link to your website. Use LinkedIn regularly to expand your professional presence among potential clients.

- Network online by joining LinkedIn groups related to proofreading, writing and editing. Ask group members how they found their first clients, and if they know of any current opportunities.

- Find other seasoned freelance proofreaders, and send a personal message asking for tips on getting started. Someone might be willing to refer you or share work with you, if they are overloaded.

- Sign up for LinkedIn Profinder to submit bids for freelance work.

## Finding Freelance Work

As a new freelancer, you must market yourself and take advantage of every opportunity to find clients. Freelance job websites where you post profiles or bid for contracts can help you find work fairly quickly. Some of these platforms operate like dating services by matching you with clients for a monthly fee.

First, subscribe to free platforms like fiverr.com. Competing for clients in the marketplace might be time consuming, but will eventually yield good results, if you offer services that are in demand.

**Begin searching for freelance work on these sites:**

www.fiverr.com

www.upwork.com

www.freelancer.com

www.peopleperhour.com

www.nexxt.com

www.guru.com

www.hireable.com

www.writeraccess.com

## Freelancing Associations

As part of their membership fees, some freelance associations might provide service listings in their directories. Some might post your profile on their website.

If you cannot specifically find organizations for proofreading, try widening your search to include freelance writing or copyediting groups.

## Start Local

Before spending money on expensive social media ads, introduce yourself to local businesses through email query letters or phone calls.

Contact community colleges, libraries, magazine or book publishers, newspapers, churches, non-profit groups, advertising and communication agencies, printing presses, office suppliers, writers and self-published authors.

# Chapter 10
# Marketing Strategies

Now that we have discussed how *you* can personally find freelance work, let's consider how *clients* will find you and discover your business.

How will you get the word out about your freelance services? You need to develop a traditional and social media marketing plan. Unfortunately, this is where many small businesses fail. You might be the best proofreader in the world, but if no one knows about you, being the best does not amount to much.

Use the strategies in this chapter to motivate and inspire you to increase your exposure with as little financial expense as possible. Remember, the goal is to make money by tapping into a consistent flow of paying customers.

## SEO Your Website

SEO stands for search engine optimization. It is a system by which companies like Google or Yahoo catalog and display websites to users who type in certain keywords. The text content on your website needs to contain words and phrases that people are researching.

"Proofreading tips," or "online proofreaders" need to appear somewhere on your site, if these terms appear in the search boxes.

Submit your site information to Google Search Console. Also, link a Google Analytics ID to the metadata of your website to get indexed, which increases your chances of getting found when people search for proofreading services. You can learn to do this yourself, contact your web designer or an SEO expert.

## Start a Blog

Blogging is a popular marketing strategy that yields great results for business owners who consistently post engaging content. Establishing a blog can mean free advertising for your business, and can even attract national product sponsors. At the very least, a blog will drive traffic to your website. Google's Blogger.com automatically indexes your posts within the Google search engine, which increases exposure to your website.

## Work Samples

Instead of simply telling people what you can do, show them! If you edited a few articles in the past, post a before and after document to your website —a copy of the article before your edits and after your edits. If you do not have client samples, create mock-ups to show what you can do, if hired.

## Business Cards

Now that you have established your company name, phone, services and website address, have you ordered business cards yet? Business cards are an inexpensive necessity for your marketing efforts. When you attend networking events or casually mention your business in the checkout line, you must give people a snapshot of your business and a way to contact you, which is the benefit of keeping business cards in your wallet, purse or pocket at all times.

## Join the Chamber of Commerce

Most cities in the United States sponsor a local chamber of commerce that supports the success of large and small businesses in the state. Members often receive exclusive access to networking events, workshops, and other opportunities for an annual fee. Search your city's website to locate a chapter near you.

## Networking

Get out of your office! Meet people in person. In addition to chamber of commerce events, attend free workshops or presentations at local libraries. Find local chapters of professional organizations dedicated to writers, editors, authors or public relations professionals who might be looking for good freelance proofreaders.

## Employment Ads

Businesses that need proofreaders or editors often post classified ads in local newspapers or through online job boards. Scour job sites like indeed.com for listings. Even if the position is full-time or in-house, you can still boldly offer your proofreading services, until the position is filled. Who knows? You might land long-term contract work. It never hurts to ask.

## Meetup Groups

*Meetup* is a social networking site that matches people to event and volunteer opportunities in their local area. You might be surprised at how many special interest groups have been formed in your community for writers, book buffs, editors, hikers, wine enthusiasts...the listings are endless. Since it is free to join and create groups, you might consider hosting a local mixer for fellow freelancers or communications professionals.

## Toastmasters Meetings

*Toastmasters* is an international organization with thousands of chapters around the world dedicated to improving speech writing and oral presentation skills. Basically, local members write speeches and present them before the group for critique. You could ask permission to speak about your services, even if you do not join the group.

## Public Speaking

Hustle your speaking skills. Try your hand at creating an interesting presentation that stresses the importance of good, error-free writing in the workplace. Otherwise, choose a current topic of interest to business owners or employees. Give the presentation a catchy title to pique interest.

Contact local business associations, libraries, or human resource professionals at large and small corporations about delivering your presentation. The exposure could generate new clients.

## Webinars

You could also turn your presentation into a free online workshop, live or pre-recorded. People love webinars! Webinars broaden your reach beyond your local area, which is great for freelancers who primarily work remotely without ever meeting clients face-to-face. You can also post a recording of the webinar on your website to drive additional traffic to your home page.

## Teaching or Training

Do you have experience teaching adult learners? Serving as an adjunct teacher at a community college or adult learning center is an excellent way to increase your exposure among a broad range of people from different walks of life. Some students might be well connected. If traditional teaching is not an option for you, how about developing a one-hour proofreading workshop that includes lots of interaction and hands-on exercises? You could charge a minimum of $25 per person to generate immediate income and future clients.

## Newsletters

If you have the time and interest, you could create your own newsletter. Choose a focus that is related to your freelance business and provides relevant, valuable information. You can distribute a monthly newsletter to an email list, or publish it directly to your website. When you post the link to your social media accounts, readers will be directed to your website where they can also learn more about you and your services.

Instead of creating a newsletter, you can scout companies and organizations that regularly publish newsletters. Of course, they need a proofreader! So, pitch your services to these organizations. You can often find community newsletters at grocery stores, library lobbies, local restaurants or coffee shops.

## Podcasting

At the time of this writing, podcasting is all the rage, because a lucky few actually earn thousands of dollars in sponsorships for their podcasts. Since the podcast market is so saturated, you really have to tackle compelling topics in a unique way to get noticed. Instead of focusing on proofreading or life as a freelancer, you might need to scan related topics like how to side-hustle your way through bouts of unemployment. Think informative and inspirational.

Podcasting requires some degree of skill with audio production. Do you have the equipment to record your voice into an audio editing program? Can you clean and edit the audio so that it sounds good to listeners? Can you insert music, interviews or sound bites into the audio? Can you post your final audio to an online podcast platform for all to hear?

Creating a podcast is time intensive and involves a steep learning curve, especially if you have never recorded one before. However, you could find established podcasts related to your business, and ask the host to interview you as a guest. In this way, you still get podcast publicity without the hassle of all the extra work.

## Volunteering

Actually, working for free can be profitable. While donating your time and talents to helping others, you might connect with influential people who can advance your business. Grant-funded non-profit groups write tons of proposals that could benefit from professional proofreading services.

## Introductory Query Letters

Yes, break out your good stationery, stamps and white #10 business envelopes. We are going old school with this strategy!

Of course, email (electronic mail) is the fastest most popular way to contact potential clients. However, filters and spam blockers might send your email to the trash folder without reaching its intended recipient.

With this in mind, you can launch a two-pronged marketing attack on local business owners, HR managers, college deans, or any authority figure who might be able hire you. Send your letter via email first.

If you get no response, wait three days, and send a printed copy of the letter through snail mail. Even if you do get declined by someone via email, get bold and mail the letter anyway, but without a specific person's name.

A letter addressed to *Department Training Manager* might get routed to an assistant who might forward your information to a better prospect within the company.

**Your error-free, professionally written letter must be:**

- clear, brief
- persuasive, specific

If you are just starting out, do not mention that you are brand new or inexperienced. Do not discuss price or payment in the letter. Do not ask for a meeting, but encourage them to contact you.

In your letter, do not try to be clever, cute or funny. Remain straight forward and professional. Believe it or not, some people might actually get offended by your attempts to be personable.

**See the example letter on the next page.**

## Example: Introductory Letter

Potential Client Name
Company
Address
Date

### Freelance proofreader and copyeditor now available to support your team.

Dear _____,

Do you want to ensure that every report, brochure, newsletter, white paper, grant or any other important document you send displays excellent grammar and high-quality business writing, with no mistakes?

My name is _____, and I am a local proofreader and copyeditor now accepting freelance assignments for documents of any length.

I provide fast and effective service with on-time delivery. In addition to proofreading, I have many years of writing and college teaching experience as an English instructor. My extensive background and skills complement any communications department or project that needs cost-effective assistance.

Please contact me to discuss your current or future writing, editing or proofreading needs.

Sincerely,


Your Name, Your Title
Your Contact Information

# Chapter 11
# Expand Your Services

Proofreaders do not generate as much money as editors. Proofreading is the very last step of the writing process that adds a final polish to previously edited documents.

Editing often requires some degree of rewriting and reorganization of material, which takes more time and skill, and therefore, costs more money. In fact, many proofreaders also function as copyeditors.

Most clients naturally assume that a proofreader will fix every error in the document, which is what editors do. So, proofreading and copyediting are technically two different services and skillsets, but the two go hand-in-hand. Proofreaders need to be good copyeditors in order to increase profits and clientele.

Additionally, proofreaders and copyeditors need to be good writers. All of these services complement each other, because each is essential to the writing process. Have you written any articles as a freelance writer? Writers generally command higher fees than copyeditors and proofreaders, because the art of writing is so personal and time intensive, as well as physically and emotionally draining.

In order to receive as much money as possible, your proofreading side-hustle needs to expand to a small business that offers:

- copywriting services
- copyediting services
- proofreading services

This trifecta of services can be extremely profitable, especially if you target the one thing many business professionals will pay you for like résumé writing. Instead of trying to write, edit or proofread every kind of document in all the world, focus on two or three document types for two or three industries.

## Maximize Your Writing Skills

For example, you can write résumés for teachers transitioning out of education into corporate jobs. Once you focus your efforts, you can increase your business faster than you think.

## Profitable Side-Hustles

In addition to writing, editing and proofreading, you might also consider maximizing your writing skills and expanding your freelance business into other profitable arenas.

## eBook Publishing

People pay good money for relevant information on a variety of subjects. Do you remember Matthew

Lesko? Back in the early 90's, Mr. Lesko wore wild, colorful suits on television, and ran infomercials about getting grant and scholarship funds from the federal government.

At the time of this writing, he is 76 years-old and sells informational reports as eBooks on his website for $4.95. One in particular, *"101 Best Grants to Start or Expand a Business"* might be of interest to you.

So, in addition to his mentoring services and other products, he offers low-cost reports such as these in the form of eBooks. Years later, customers still buy the information he sells that center on one topic: federal grant funding. Let his example be a lesson to us all.

## Consulting

Consulting requires time to meet with people one-on-one either by phone, video chat or face-to-face. As a paid consultant, you must deliver results. Clearly define the one thing you will help clients complete, produce or improve.

Depending on your subject matter, experience, education and qualifications, you could charge $30-$150 per hour.

## Presentation Creator

PowerPoint presentations rule the business world. Unfortunately, many professionals do not have time to complete their own presentations for sales meetings, employee trainings or conventions. As a highly skilled, creative freelancer, you can offer to develop slide decks for busy professionals.

## Self-publishing

You can write books on bankable topics, and self-publish your work. Depending on your subject, you can generate income sooner than most other authors. However, you could also help authors who want to self-publish a book with writing, editing and proofreading. Instead of creating your own books, consulting with authors might generate more immediate income.

## Newsletter Publisher

Several businesses and non-profits publish in-house newsletters. An insurance company, for example, might produce monthly or quarterly newsletters that can benefit from freelance editing services.

## Web Content Provider

Content marketing is king, but writing content takes lots of time and consistent effort. You could provide bloggers and businesses with compelling articles to keep readers and customers engaged.

## Local Publishing

A local technical writer launched a niche, 10-page guide for businesses in her county. She sold advertising that featured their professional services. The publication grew into a rudimentary blog site that strictly focuses on news, events and businesses in her county. She was eventually able to quit her full-time job. You could do the same.

## How-to Guides

You can strictly focus on writing and selling how-to articles for different industries, such as "How to Start a Podcast." Perhaps you can bundle them as eBooks or sell them individually by the page. Either way, content sells.

## Corporate Writer

Ghostwriting for high-powered executives can be quite lucrative. What if a CEO wants to self-publish a book on everyday finance, but does not have the time or ability to produce this book? If you are willing to spend 4-6 months on a project, you might thrive in this field. Other than that, corporations always need annual reports, white papers and all kinds of technical business documents.

## Special Skills

Bear in mind that most of these additional services require high levels of writing, editing, proofreading and intermediate graphic design skills.

# Freelance Rate Sheet

| TYPE OF WORK | ESTIMATED PACE | RANGE OF FEES |
|---|---|---|
| Basic Copyediting | 5-10 pgs/hr | $30-$40/hr |
| Heavy Copyediting | 2-5 pgs/hr | $40-$50/hr |
| Website Copyediting | N/A | $40-$50/hr |
| Developmental Editing | 1-5 pgs/hr | $45-$55/hr |
| Substantive/Line Editing | 1-6 pgs/hr | $40-$60/hr |
| Newsletters | N/A | $40-$100/hr |
| Proofreading | 9-13 pgs/hr | $30-$35/hr |
| Ghostwriting | 1-3 pgs/hr | $50-$60/hr .26-.50c/word |
| Grant/Proposal/Sales PR Writing | 1-3 pgs/hr | $50-$60/hr .30-.95c/word |
| Blog Article/Feature Writing | 1-3 pgs/hr | $40-$50/hr .26-.50c/word |
| General Business/Professional Writing | 1-3 pgs/hr | $40-$100/hr .20-$2/word |
| Technical/Trade Writing | 1-3 pgs/hr | $50-$60/hr .45-.55c/word |

Adapted from the Editorial Freelancers Association.
www.the-efa.org

# Resources

Hampton, Ashan R. *Proofreading Power Skills &
Drills: Become an Effective Proofreader.* Cornerstone
Publishing/Lulu.com. 2018. Print.

Sheldon, George. *Start Your Own Freelance
Writing Business and More.* Canada:
Entrepreneur Press. 2008. Print.

# Index

Made in the USA
Monee, IL
30 March 2021

64272572R00056